Vehicles On The Move

AIRCRAFT CARRIERS
Runways at Sea

MANHATTAN

Lynn Peppas

🌳 Crabtree Publishing Company

www.crabtreebooks.com

Created by Bobbie Kalman

Author
Lynn Peppas

Editor
Adrianna Morganelli

Proofreader
Kathy Middleton

Photo research
Samara Parent

Design
Samara Parent

Production coordinator
and prepress technician
Samara Parent

Print coordinator
Katherine Berti

Photographs
Dreamstime: pages 8–9
Shutterstock: back cover, pages 1, 3, 4–5, 10–11, 12, 16, 24 (top)
U.S. Navy: photo by PM3 Dusty Howell, March 15, 2005: front cover; photo by Mass Communication Specialist 3rd Class Travis K. Mendoza: page 6 (top); photo by Mass Communication Specialist Seaman Leonard Adams: page 6 (bottom); photo by Mass Communication Specialist 1st Class Brien Aho: page 7 (top); photo by Mass Communication Specialist 2nd Class John P. Curtis: page 14; photo by Mass Communication Specialist 1st Class David McKee: page 15; photo by Mass Communication Specialist 2nd Class Brooks B. Patton Jr.: page 21; photo by Mass Communication Specialist 1st Class Jason Winn: pages 22–23; photo by Mass Communication Specialist 2nd Class Chris Williamson: page 24 (bottom)
Wikimedia Commons: Gaetano56: pages 18–19; David Hume Kennerly, White House: page 30; U.S. Government: page 13; U.S. Navy: pages 6–7, 17, 20, 24, 26–27, 28–29, 31

Front cover: The Nimitz-class aircraft carrier, USS Carl Vinson, is under way in the Indian Ocean.
Back cover: The USS *Midway* is docked in San Diego, California.
Title page: The USS *Nimitz* arrives in Bremerton, Washington.

Library and Archives Canada Cataloguing in Publication

Peppas, Lynn
    Aircraft carriers : runways at sea / Lynn Peppas.

(Vehicles on the move)
Includes index.
Issued also in electronic formats.
ISBN 978-0-7787-2747-7 (bound).--ISBN 978-0-7787-2752-1 (pbk.)

    1. Aircraft carriers--Juvenile literature.
I. Title. II. Series: Vehicles on the move

V874.P46 2011   j623.825'5   C2011-906712-9

Library of Congress Cataloging-in-Publication Data

Peppas, Lynn.
Aircraft carriers : runways at sea / Lynn Peppas.
    p. cm. -- (Vehicles on the move)
Includes index.
ISBN 978-0-7787-2747-7 (reinforced library binding : alk. paper) --
ISBN 978-0-7787-2752-1 (pbk. : alk. paper) -- ISBN 978-1-4271-9925-6
(electronic pdf) -- ISBN 978-1-4271-9930-0 (electronic html)
1. Aircraft carriers--Juvenile literature. I. Title. II. Series.

V874.P47 2012
623.825'5--dc23
                                                         2011039689

Crabtree Publishing Company

www.crabtreebooks.com   1-800-387-7650

Printed in the U.S.A./112011/JA20111018

Published in Canada
Crabtree Publishing
616 Welland Ave.
St. Catharines, Ontario
L2M 5V6

Published in the United States
Crabtree Publishing
PMB 59051
350 Fifth Avenue, 59th Floor
New York, New York 10118

Published in the United Kingdom
Crabtree Publishing
Maritime House
Basin Road North, Hove
BN41 1WR

Published in Australia
Crabtree Publishing
3 Charles Street
Coburg North
VIC 3058

Contents

Aircraft Carrier

Aircraft carriers are **military** vehicles that carry aircraft such as jets. Vehicles are machines that carry people and things from one place to another. An aircraft carrier is a ship with a **runway** for aircraft to take off and land on. Ship are vehicles that float, and aircraft are vehicles that fly.

An aircraft carrier is also called a warship. They are very expensive military vehicles.

Sometimes a country's **armed forces** need to have aircraft close to another country that is far away. Aircraft carriers bring the aircraft and pilots to where they need to go. The carrier also acts as an **air base** for aircraft and crew to stay and operate from.

Parts of an Aircraft Carrier

Aircraft carriers come in different sizes depending on the jobs they do. The flight deck is the flat surface of the carrier where aircraft take off and land. The deck is about the size of four and a half football fields (18,000 square meters). Officers give orders from the bridge. The bridge is part of a building called the island on top of the deck .

engine room

bridge

island

hangar bay

Above: *USS* **George H.W. Bush**

There are seven decks, or levels, below the flight deck. Aircraft are stored below the flight deck in the **hangar**. The engine room holds the engines and the **power source** that makes the ship move. There are also rooms, or quarters, for the crew members that work aboard the ship to sleep.

jet blast deflectors

catapult

crew quarters

flight deck

hull

Working on an Aircraft Carrier

Some aircraft carriers need more than 5,000 people to do different jobs. They live, eat, sleep, and work on an aircraft carrier for months at a time. People who work on the flight deck wear different colored vests or shirts to show what job they do. The flight deck is a busy and dangerous place to work.

Many people who work on an aircraft carrier do not go on the flight deck or island. They work inside the ship and do not get to see sunlight often. An aircraft carrier needs doctors, dentists, and even barbers onboard.

Sometimes aircraft carriers are described as being like a city at sea.

Blue shirts help handle the aircraft on the flight deck.

Yellow shirts direct aircraft coming in or taking off.

Aircraft captains wear brown shirts.

Green shirts are for those who work on an aircraft's takeoff or landing gear.

Workers who fuel the aircraft wear purple.

People who handle the weapons wear red.

The safety crew wears white.

Take Off!

Today, most flight decks are over 1,000 feet (305 m) long. That is still not long enough for most military aircraft to take off from. A machine called a catapult helps the aircraft take off from the ship. The catapult gives the aircraft an extra boost of power so it can go very fast over a short distance.

jet blast deflector

This jet is hooked up to the catapult and is ready to take off.

The flight crew puts up the jet blast **deflector** before a jet takes off. A deflector is a fence or wall that bends the hot jet **exhaust** upward. This keeps other aircraft and people nearby safe from the jet's heat.

A member of the catapult crew watches as a jet takes off.

Coming in for a Landing

Most military aircraft have a hook at the back of the tail. As the jet lands on the ship, the tailhook catches on a large, steel cable attached to the flight deck. This cable, called an **arresting** wire, helps the jet stop quickly.

Landing signal officers use radio handsets, which look like telephones, to talk to pilots and help them land safely.

There are four cables stretched across the deck. When the jet hooks onto one of these cables, the aircraft can stop in seconds. Landing an aircraft on an aircraft carrier is one of the hardest jobs for a pilot to do.

An arresting wire can stop a 54,000-pound (24,494 kg) aircraft going 150 mph (240 km/h) in two seconds.

Aircraft on Aircraft Carriers

Special aircraft called carrier planes work from an aircraft carrier. Some have folding wings to save space in the hangar. Some aircraft carrier hangars can hold up to 100 aircraft. Special elevators move the aircraft to and from the flight deck on top.

Aircraft fills the hanger of the USS Ronald Reagan.

Some aircraft, such as the Hornet fighter jet, are designed specifically to work from an aircraft carrier. Military helicopters such as the Seahawk can easily take off and land on a carrier because they can **hover**. Another fighter jet called the Harrier looks like a jet but can move and hover like a helicopter.

An AV-8B Harrier lands aboard the USS Makin Island, *an amphibious assault ship.*

Onboard Weapons

Aircraft carriers are one of the most expensive military vehicles. They are extremely large and cost **billions** of dollars to build. Because of their size, aircraft carriers cannot move quickly to avoid **enemy** attack. They need weapons for protection.

Some carriers have **missile** launchers, as well as a defensive weapon system nicknamed Sea Whiz. Sea Whiz has guns and cannons to shoot at enemy missiles or aircraft. Aircraft carriers also have a defense system to protect them from torpedo attack. A torpedo is a bomb that travels through water.

The name Sea Whiz comes from CIWS, which stands for Close-In Weapon System.

Light Aircraft Carriers

A light aircraft carrier is a smaller military ship that carries aircraft. Some fighter jets such as the Harrier do not need a long runway for takeoff or landing. That is because they can take off or land vertically, or straight up or down, like a helicopter can.

A light aircraft carrier needs a much smaller crew than a large carrier. It takes a crew of about 5,000 to 6,000 people to operate a large carrier. A light aircraft carrier needs a crew of only about 1,000.

A light aircraft carrier can travel at speeds of up to 32 mph (52 km/h).

Fleet Carriers

A fleet is a group of warships that travel and work together. A fleet carrier is the most important warship in a fleet because it carries the attack aircraft. It is the largest and most expensive ship in the group.

This is a fleet of aircraft carriers on display. In battle, the ships would be farther apart.

The world's longest warship is the American aircraft carrier USS *Enterprise*. It was the first **nuclear**-powered aircraft carrier ever built. This warship has won many awards over its 50 years on the seas.

The USS Enterprise *is 1,123 feet (342 m) long and can hold up to 90 aircraft.*

Supercarriers

Supercarriers are the largest aircraft carriers on the seas. They weigh over 100,000 tons (90,700 metric tons). They measure over 1,000 feet (305 m) in length and travel at speeds over 35 mph (56 km/h). It carries 90 aircraft and runs on nuclear power.

Every warship has its own motto, or saying. The motto of the USS George H.W. Bush is "Freedom at Work."

The USS *George H.W. Bush* is a supercarrier that was built in 2006. It was named after the 41st president of the United States, George H. W. Bush. He flew aircraft from a carrier in World War II.

Anti-Submarine Carriers

An anti-submarine warfare carrier is sometimes called an ASW carrier. ASW are the first three letters of anti-submarine warfare. It is a small aircraft carrier used to hunt and destroy enemy submarines. A submarine is a boat that travels under water at great depths.

Submarines shoot torpedoes and missiles. They are a threat to ships and aircraft carriers at sea.

The *Giuseppe Garibaldi* is an ASW carrier from Italy. It fires missiles and torpedoes. It carries Harrier jets and Augusta attack helicopters.

Helicopter Carriers

A helicopter carrier is a light aircraft carrier. They are sometimes called destroyers. These ships carry attack helicopters and transport helicopters. They also carry soldiers and their weapons.

Japan's two largest helicopter carriers used in combat are the Hyūga (above) and the Ise.

The *Ise* is a helicopter carrier from Japan. It is over 587 feet (179 m) long. It travels at speeds up to 35 mph (56 km/h). It carries weapons such as missiles and torpedoes. It also carries up to 11 helicopters.

Amphibious Assault Carriers

Amphibious means something that can move in water or on land. An amphibious assault carrier is a ship that carries aircraft, landing craft, and hovercraft. Landing craft are vehicles that carry soldiers from the ship to an enemy shore. A hovercraft is a vehicle that is able to move on land or water on a cushion of air.

An amphibious assault carrier has a well deck, which is a large door at the back of a ship. The ship takes on water to flood the well deck. Hovercraft or landing craft enter or leave the ship through the well deck door.

Future Aircraft Carriers

The United States Navy is working on making bigger and better supercarriers. This class of aircraft carrier is called the Gerald R. Ford class. The class is named after Gerald R. Ford who was the 38th president of the United States. Gerald Ford fought in the Navy in World War II on an aircraft carrier before he became president.

The ship USS *Gerald R. Ford* will be the first supercarrier in its class. It is being built in Hampton Roads, Virginia. It should set sail by 2015. It will cost over 5 billion dollars.

Glossary

air base The main area of military operations, storage of aircraft, and living quarters for flight crew

armed forces A country's group of soldiers who fight on the ground, at sea, and in the air

arresting Bringing to a stop

billion A very large number equal to one thousand millions

deflector A solid object that moves, or pushes, the flow of air coming toward it

enemy A force that works against a person or a country

exhaust The gas and waste products from an engine

hangar A large shed used to store things such as aircraft

hover To stay in one place in the air

military A country's armed forces

missile An explosive weapon that is shot at a target in the distance

nuclear An energy source that is made from a nuclear reaction

power source The kind of energy used to run a ship

runway A strip of ground used by aircraft to take off or land on

Index

```
J          Peppas, Lynn.
623.825
P          Aircraft carriers.


$26.60
```

```
J          Peppas, Lynn.
623.825
P          Aircraft
             carriers.


$26.60
```

DATE	BORROWER'S NAME	

4/12

BAKER & TAYLOR